How to really attract money

How to really attract money

Jasmin Hajro

Jasmin Hajro
© 2021 Jasmin Hajro
All rights reserved.
Written by Jasmin Hajro
Translated by Jasmin Hajro
Selfpublished by Jasmin Hajro
Cover design by Jasmin Hajro
First edition 2021

Contents :

First part of book Victories, also known as book Victory
and
Book the Great King
Booklet How to really attract money
Book How to build your fortune

Whitepaper : How to really attract money

Hello,
how are you doing ?
What is your age ?
Do you go to school or are you already working?
Perhaps you started your own business….
Thank you for choosing one of my books to read
This is a box set with 5 booklets in 1 book.

Do you have some money in your wallet or pocket?
Pull it out ,
put it down on the table before you….
The bills and coins….

Now go to another room in the house
and think continually about that money that you left on the table in the other room…
think of getting it, attracting it…
visualize it coming to you….
Do this very seriously……………

See ?

Nothing happens….

The bills and coins are dead or not alive matter….

Yes I know the messages about the Law of Attraction
and ´teachers ´ who preach about manifesting abundance…

I am 36 years old,
I have had several different jobs,
and now I run my 2nd company ,called Hajro, like my last name.
I sell greeting cards, door to door , and the books that I have written I sell online.

Never in my life have I attracted money,
not once in those 36 years of living and working about 10 years,
never have coins and bills floated to me….

´Money doesn´t move on its own´

Only people can move money from one pocket to another…

So you better focus on attracting people who have some money…

You can do that by marketing yourself and your skills
Maybe you can sell a product or service, and then you market and advertize that…

The only way that I attracted money to me was by working for it,
you will also only attract money ,by working for it….

Sorry to burst the bubble,
but it was bullshit anyway,
and you deserve the truth…

People only attract or accumulate money by working for it.

So spend your days working for money
and not visualizing it ,floating to you

Build your Fortune

The bio of author Jasmin Hajro, nice to meet you

Hello dear reader, how are you ?

Thank you for buying one of my books.

My name is Jasmin Hajro,
I was born on July 6, 1985 in Bosnia.
As refugees, we came to the Netherlands 21 years ago.
After having completed school & worked at several jobs ...

On 17 December 2012, I founded my first company:

investment firm Jasko. After a successful first year,
I unfortunately had to close that company.

After a short period of rest, unemployment and temporary work.
I started again as an entrepreneur.

On September 1, 2015, I founded establishment Hajro.

(We say establishment instead of company,
because we do a bit more then just sell stuff.
Like providing jobs,
donating to 40 different charities,
and helping people to live richer.)

Since the beginning the core activity is,
selling sets of greeting cards,
door to door.
Nowadays the product range has been expanded.

With, among other things, the selling of my 12 books.

The royalties of my books are donated to the charity:
foundation Giveth Life.
From there more than 15 other charities
receive donations.
And by buying this book, so do you.
Thank you.

My company website is www.hajro-international.webnode.nl

For more information about my company

& the foundation, go to www.jasminhajro.com

How this book came into existence

In 2007 I started working at a restaurant, as a dishwasher. I lived with my mother and had no living expenses. I earned about 1000,- euro per month. So I had enough money in savings. At my work I learned to work in the kitchen & worked my way up.

Then I learned that my saving were not actually growing with the interest, because inflation was as high as my interest.

I did a home course called Wiser with money.
Then home course Stock exchanges and investing.
I read books on finance.
Somewhere I learned that for retirement :
If you live in a foreign country for a couple of years or are an immigrant

When you retire, you will get a pension cut.

Because you don't have a complete employment history of 47 years.

This meant that my parents were screwed, when they retire.
(Becaues they are immigrants, and will only have worked in the Netherlands for about 20 years.)
How would they survive with a half pension ?
When they're old and can't work anymore, and when they should be enjoying life.

Then I decided to become rich.
I had to, so I can give them a decent

pension.

So I went on with educating myself on finance.

Read more book on finance.

Started investing,

in mutual funds, bonds, stocks.

Made some profit & also lost some money.

No problem, I was lerning.

But I was exhausting myself,

because I also worked fulltime in the kitchen.

So I started looking for a better way,

that would cost me less time & energy.

And thru thinking about how to do it better.

I came up with a system.

When I started a company to invest

professionally for clients,

I applied for a patent.

To protect my financial system.

(It's kind out outside the intention of this book. But If you want to know what happened. My company Jasko had 1600,- euro in the portfolio. If I made a 20% return on that, I could pay the promised return
to my clients, which I did, and buy a present for myself.
But it was not enough to make a living.
And then I also had no clue about selling,
which is required to get new clients.
And I had to close the company.
Which hurted, because it was my baby.
But I have the experience.)

Now I have received the patent

for my invention

the financial system.

You can see it at the next page.

Well...

I gave you my bio,

so that you know me a little better.

I have told you how & why

this book came into existence.

And now is the time for you to read

the book.

Remember that I write Doing books,

which means that I describe actions that you

can take and from them get results.

Don't worry, it doesn't take a lot of your

time. And I have kept it simple.

The good news

Money keeps flowing into your life.
Money continues to flow.
Money keeps circulating.
Money has done this for hundreds of years.
Money will continue to do this for hundreds of years.

Since you first received pocket money,
since you were paid for your first job.
Since your studentloan money began to come in,
since your job started paying your monthly salary.
Since your business became profitable.

Money kept flowing into your life every month.

Even to people with social wellfare.
Thank God.
Fortunately money keeps coming in regularly.

There is enough money in the world.
Should it be necessary, than more money will be made.

the Pay Yourself First rule

It means that when you receive your money,
you first pay yourself.
For example by saving 10% of it.

To clarify the result,
we will make an example calculation.

For example, you earn 3000 dollars per month.
And you pay yourself first,
in other words: you save 10% of your income.
That is 300, - dollar per month.

A year has 12 months,
So after 1 year you have
(12 x 300) = 3600, - dollar.
After 1 year you have saved a whole month's salary.

If you save 10% every month,
how much will you have after 10 years?
(3600 x 10) = 36000 dollar.

So after 10 years you'll have 36000 dollars
or a whole year's salary in your savingsaccount.

Later on in this book,
you'll see how to make that money that you save every month.
Grow faster.

10% of everything

It is important that when you first pay yourself,
by saving 10%.
That you save 10% of everything.

Of course 10% of your income.

But also 10% of the tip if you get it,
also 10% of your allowances,
also 10% of your gift money,
also 10% of your 13th month,
also 10% of your bonus,
also 10% of your wage increase,
also 10% of your tax refund,
also 10% of your welcome premium.

From which angle or from whom you receive money,

the first thing you do is pay yourself first.

By saving 10% of it.

the secret of success

The secret of success is Persistence.

If it takes 20 years,
for you to become a millionaire.
If that means that it requires of you
20 years,
of working and saving & investing.
Then you have to Persist 20 years with
working and saving & investing.

And not quitting after 5 years ....

PERSIST until you reach your goal.

The 2nd secret of success is:

WHAT YOU DO WITH YOUR TIME

So do not go watch TV for hours,

but start earning money

&

deal with people who earn a lot of money.

So that you learn from them to earn even more money.

That money will start to work hard for you,

according to this system,

that you are learning.

The person who will make you rich,

the one who will build your Fortune,

is YOU.

Therefore, take good care of yourself.

So you can keep on persisting

for a long time,

until you reach your goal.

Trend

Because people live longer nowadays,
they need money for a longer period of time.

Many people build up income for later,
with dividend paying &
interest-bearing investments.

This will increase the value of those kind of investments,
over time.

The part of your money
that you are going to invest,
will grow because of this trend.

Bonds explained

If you buy a bond,
you actually lend money to a company or government.
You get interest for this,
which is paid to you annually.

A bond usually costs around a thousand dollar.
Some bonds have a certain duration,
for example 10 years.
If this bond gives 5% interest,
with a duration time of 10 years.
And you buy this bond.

Then you get the upcoming 10 years,
50 dollar in interest each year.
After that 10 years, you get your deposit,
that thousand dollar back.

Some bonds have no duration in years mentioned.
There is a P mentioned, the abbreviation for Perpetual,
which means eternal.
These perpetual bonds pay interest annually, for eternity.
As long as the organization that issues them still exists.
That can be hundreds of years.

You buy a bond once,
and get 50 dollar in interest each year,
for the next 50 years or longer.
Without having to do anything else for it!

That's better, is it not?

Preparation

Before you start building your own Fortune,
we must do the preparation first.
The preparation consists of 3 things.

1. Have your will prepared by a notary.

This is not fun, but important.
So that when you're gone,
there are no ambiguities or misunderstandings.
About what you leave behind and to whom.

2. Make sure you are well insured.

Get the insurances that you need,
and think that you will need.
Such as a term life insurance policy and
a funeral insurance.
So that when you're gone,
your surviving relatives do not get stuck with those costs.
And still have to arrange things.
But that everything is already well arranged.

Try to get all your insurance policies from 1 or 2 providers, so that you get a discount on your insurance package.

3. Open the following 3 accounts:

1 A savings account,
2 a deposit account,
3 an investment account.

(Note : with deposit account is meant a bankingaccount on which you can fix an savingsamount of money, for 1 to 20 years. Which pays you interest annually, and gives back your savingsamount, after the duration period ends, which you pick. If you want your savingsamount back before duration ends, you get a fine.)

Systematically building it up

You will systematically on these 3 accounts,
build your Own Fortune.
With the amount of your income,
that you save every month.

If you, like in our previous example,
save per month 300 dollar.
Then you divide that 300 dollar,
about your 3 bankingaccounts.
1/3 Saving, so you put 100 dollar in your savings account.
1/3 Deposit, so you put 100 dollar in your deposit account.
1/3 Investing, so you put 100 dollar in your investment account.

Half of your investment account money, you invest in a
dividend yielding mutual fund.
And the other half you invest in an interest yielding bonds
mutual fund.

For example :

50 dollar in the NN Utilities Fund Dis
50 dollar in the Triodos Sustainable Bond Fund

You can leave it that way, all year round.
Without having to worry about it.

After that year, you will receive interest from your savings account.
And interest from your deposit account.

And dividend & interest from your investment account.

This money works for you now.
That's how you let it grow.
You also get over the years,
the interest on interest effect.
Which makes it grow faster.

Every month

Next month you pay yourself first,
by saving 10% of your income.

This amount of 300 dollar you divide again over your 3 bankingaccounts.
1/3 Saving, so 100 dollar into your savings account.
1/3 Deposit, so 100 dollar into your deposit account.
1/3 Investing, so 100 dollar into your investment account.

Half of your investment account money,
you invest in a dividend yielding real estate mutual fund.
The other half you invest in an interest yielding bonds mutual fund.

For example :

50 dollar in the BNP High Income Property Fund
50 dollar in the NN Global Bond Fund

In total you have:

200 dollar in your Savings account.
200 dollar in your Deposit account.
200 dollar in your investment account
The money in your investment account is
equally divided over 4 mutual funds.

This means for you,
that you receive annual interest on your savings account.
And that you receive annual interest on your deposit account.
And that your receive annual dividend &
interest on your investment account.

Every year.

The next month you do the same 3 steps again
Step 1: You save 10% of your income.

Step 2: That 10%, in our example that 300 dollar, you divide over your 3 accounts.

A third into your savings account.
A third into your deposit account.
And a third into your investment account.

Step 3: The amount that goes into your investment account, you divide in two.
One half you invest in a dividend yielding mutual fund
or
a dividend yielding real estate mutual fund.
The other half you invest in an interest yielding bonds mutual fund.

The next month you do the same 3 steps again.

Then you do the same 3 steps each month.

Why not put everything in your investing account?

It is very important that you,

stick to the described dividing.
With this dividing you only risk
a third of your money.

But by having that part that you risk,
spread well.
You reduce the risk.

Mutual funds are already spread in themselves.
A mutual fund is invested in 50, 100 or more companies.

Which reduces your risk dramatically.

The amount with which you pay yourself first every month,
that 10% that you save.
Always divide it into your 3 accounts as below:
1/3 of that 10% in savingsaccount
1/3 of that 10% in depositaccount
1/3 of that 10% in investingaccount

It is wise to also, divide your investments in mutual funds
by category,
as below :

1/3 stocks mutual funds
1/3 bonds mutual funds
1/3 real estate mutual funds

Choose mutual funds that pay you dividends or interest.

It depends
It could be,
that your savings account pays the interest per month.
Or per year.
That differs per bank and savings account.

It could be that your mutual funds
pay out the dividend per quarter.
Or per year.
That differs per mutual fund.

If you open a deposit account at Rabobank,
the so-called Target Savings.
Then you can decide for yourself,
how often you put money into it,
and how much.
That is a very convenient deposit account.

It may be that other banks,
request a minimum deposit for a
deposit account.
For example 500 dollar.

If the bank where you open your deposit account,
requires a minimum deposit .
Then you can save that up monthly,
until you have enough to meet the minimum requirement and put
it in a deposit. For several years.

In our example,
you have after 5 months (5 x 100) =
500 dollar,
saved up.
You then meet the minimum requirement for a depositaccount.
And you can put 500 dollar in your depositaccount,
fixed for 10 years or more.

After 1 year

After 1 year you saved in total
3600 dollar.
(12 months x 300 = 3600 dollar)

You have done the 3 steps on a monthly basis.

Now you have:

1/3 of 3600 is 1200 dollar and that is in your savings account.
1/3 of 3600 is 1200 dollar and that is in your deposit account.
1/3 of 3600 is 1200 dollar and that is in your investment account.

You have spread your investments in mutual funds per category,
So :

1/3 of 1200 is 400 dollar and that is in stocks mutual funds.
1/3 of 1200 is 400 dollar euro and that is in bond mutual funds.
1/3 of 1200 is 400 dollar and that is in real estate mutual funds.

You have invested in mutual funds that pay out dividend and interest, to you.

So you receive interest and dividend on your investment account.
You will receive interest on your deposit account.
And you also receive interest on your savings account.

Step 4 and 5

Step 4: If you have 1200 dollar in mutual funds, you sell 1100 of it.

In our example, you have invested 1200 dollar every year in mutual funds.

So every year you sell 1100 dollar from your mutual funds.

So that you have 1100 dollar in cash, on your investment account.

Step 5: With that 1100 dollar cash on your investment account, you buy 1 individual bond.

A bond that pays a high interest rate to you, and has a long duration time.

Or a perpetual bond that pays a high interest to you.

**Note : It is forbidden for you to buy junk bonds !
Corporate and government bonds are allowed.**

Na 10 jaar

If you do the described steps,
every month and every year.
The next 10 years.

Then you will have :

1200 x 10 years = 12000 dollar on your savings account.
1200 x 10 years = 12000 dollar on your deposit account.
1200 x 10 years = 12000 dollar on your investing account.

Every time you had 1200 dollar
in mutual funds,
you sold 1100 dollars of it.
And from that cash you bought 1 bond.
So after 10 years you have 10 bonds.

If you have bought perpetual bonds,
that pay 10% interest per year,

You receive (10 x 100) = 1000 dollar in interest annually.

Well then you can buy 2 bonds per year.
From what you save and divide into your investingaccount
& from the interest payout from your bonds.

This will result in increasing your total annual receivable rturns.

Increasingly bigger annual returns for you

In the course of time, your total returns annually,
increase by the interest & dividend that you receive.
This allows you to buy more and more bonds per year.
And thus, your total annual returns
become even bigger.

For example after many years:

You have 10 perpetual bonds that pay 10% interest annually,
you receive 1000 dollar per year in interest.
And you have 100 bonds that have a duration time of 20 years,
which payout 8% interest.
You then receive 8000 dollar per year in interest.

Plus the interest that you receive on your savings account

& plus the interest that you receive on your deposit account.

In total, your annual returns are more than ten thousand dollars.

And with that you can buy more individual bonds,
so that your total annual returns
become even bigger.

**In this way,
the system is reinforcing itself,
to yield bigger annual returns for you,
every year,
for the rest of your life.**

What now & how do you proceed ?
If you understand this book,
and you understand all the steps
that you have to do.
If you are going to do everything yourself,
then that's fine.

Get started.

Start building your Fortune.

If you think you can use some help,
you can ask that someone.
You can ask your adviser at the bank.
Or you find an independent consultant.
Then you can together
Build your Fortune.

Put this book in a place,
so that you see it every day.
So that it reminds you of your goal:

Building your own Fortune.

And so it reminds you of the steps you have to do every month
& every year.

_____

Thank you for buying this book

&

good luck with

Building Your Fortune.

```
P.S. I recommend that you reread this book
          every month. To stay focused.



  If you like this book and get good value
                    from it,
     please be so kind to recommend it
          to the people that you know.

         Or sent a copy or 2 as a gift.


           So that it helps them to

           improve their lives also.


                   Thank you.
```

The bio of author Jasmin Hajro, nice to meet you

Hello dear reader, how are you ?

Thank you for buying one of my books.

My name is Jasmin Hajro,
I was born on July 6, 1985 in Bosnia.
As refugees, we came to the Netherlands 21 years ago.
After having completed school & worked at several jobs ...

On 17 December 2012, I founded my first company:
investment firm Jasko. After a successful first year,

I unfortunately had to close that company.

After a short period of rest, unemployment and temporary work.
I started again as an entrepreneur.

On September 1, 2015, I founded establishment Hajro.

(We say establishment instead of company,
because we do a bit more then just sell stuff.
Like providing jobs,
donating to 40 different charities,
and helping people to live richer.)

Since the beginning the core activity is,
selling sets of greeting cards,
door to door.
Nowadays the product range has been expanded.

With, among other things, the selling of my 12 books.

The royalties of my books are donated to the charity:
foundation Giveth Life.
From there more than 40 other charities
receive donations.
And by buying this book, so do you.
Thank you.

My company is now part of Hajro Group,
which consists of 19 different subsidiaries,
that are part of 1 umbrella organization.
Called Energy Now (Energie Nu)

For more information about my company
& the foundation, go to www.hajrobv.nl

How this book came into existence

In 2007 I started working at a restaurant, as a dishwasher. I lived with my mother and had no living expenses. I earned about 1000,- euro per month. So I had enough money in savings. At my work I learned to work in the kitchen & worked my way up. Then I learned that my saving were not actually growing with the interest, because inflation was as high as my interest.

I did a home course called Wiser with money. Then home course Stock exchanges and investing.

I read books on finance.

Somewhere I learned that for retirement : If you live in a foreign country for a couple of years or are an immigrant

When you retire, you will get a

pension cut.

Because you don't have a complete

employment history of 47 years.

This meant that my parents were

screwed, when they retire.

(Becaues they are immigrants,

and will only have worked in the Netherlands

for about 20 years.)

How would they survive with a half pension ?

When they're old and can't work anymore,

and when they should be enjoying life.

Then I decided to become rich.

I had to, so I can give them a decent

pension.

So I went on with educating myself on

finance.

Read more book on finance.

Started investing,

in mutual funds, bonds, stocks.

Made some profit & also lost some money.

No problem, I was lerning.

But I was exhausting myself,

because I also worked fulltime in the

kitchen.

So I started looking for a better way,

that would cost me less time & energy.

And thru thinking about how to do it better.

I came up with a system.

When I started a company to invest

professionally for clients,

I applied for a patent.

To protect my financial system.

(It's kind out outside the intention of this book. But If you want to know what happened. My company Jasko had 1600,- euro in the portfolio. If I made a 20% return on that, I could pay the promised return
to my clients, which I did, and buy a present for myself.
But it was not enough to make a living.
And then I also had no clue about selling,
which is required to get new clients.
And I had to close the company.
Which hurted, because it was my baby.
But I have the experience.)

Now I have received the patent

for my invention

the financial system.

You can see it at the next page.

Well...

I gave you my bio,

so that you know me a little better.

I have told you how & why

this book came into existence.

And now is the time for you to read

the book.

Remember that I write Doing books,

which means that I describe actions that you

can take and from them get results.

Don't worry, it doesn't take a lot of your

time. And I have kept it simple.

The good news

Money keeps flowing into your life.
Money continues to flow.
Money keeps circulating.
Money has done this for hundreds of years.
Money will continue to do this for hundreds of years.

Since you first received pocket money,
since you were paid for your first job.
Since your studentloan money began to come in,
since your job started paying your monthly salary.
Since your business became profitable.

Money kept flowing into your life every month.

Even to people with social wellfare.
Thank God.
Fortunately money keeps coming in regularly.

There is enough money in the world.
Should it be necessary, than more money will be made.

the Pay Yourself First rule

It means that when you receive your money,
you first pay yourself.
For example by saving 10% of it.

To clarify the result,
we will make an example calculation.

For example, you earn 3000 dollars per month.
And you pay yourself first,
in other words: you save 10% of your income.
That is 300, - dollar per month.

A year has 12 months,
So after 1 year you have
(12 x 300) = 3600, - dollar.
After 1 year you have saved a whole month's salary.

If you save 10% every month,
how much will you have after 10 years?
(3600 x 10) = 36000 dollar.

So after 10 years you'll have 36000 dollars
or a whole year's salary in your savingsaccount.

Later on in this book,
you'll see how to make that money that you save every month.
Grow faster.

10% of everything

It is important that when you first pay yourself,
by saving 10%.
That you save 10% of everything.

Of course 10% of your income.

But also 10% of the tip if you get it,
also 10% of your allowances,
also 10% of your gift money,
also 10% of your 13th month,
also 10% of your bonus,
also 10% of your wage increase,
also 10% of your tax refund,
also 10% of your welcome premium.

From which angle or from whom you receive money,

the first thing you do is pay yourself first.

By saving 10% of it.

the secret of success

The secret of success is Persistence.

If it takes 20 years,
for you to become a millionaire.
If that means that it requires of you
20 years,
of working and saving & investing.
Then you have to Persist 20 years with
working and saving & investing.

And not quitting after 5 years ....

PERSIST until you reach your goal.

The 2nd secret of success is:

WHAT YOU DO WITH YOUR TIME

So do not go watch TV for hours,

but start earning money

&

deal with people who earn a lot of money.

So that you learn from them to earn even more money.

That money will start to work hard for you,

according to this system,

that you are learning.

The person who will make you rich,

the one who will build your Fortune,

is YOU.

Therefore, take good care of yourself.

So you can keep on persisting

for a long time,

until you reach your goal.

Trend

Because people live longer nowadays,
they need money for a longer period of time.

Many people build up income for later,
with dividend paying &
interest-bearing investments.

This will increase the value of those kind of investments,
over time.

The part of your money
that you are going to invest,
will grow because of this trend.

Bonds explained

If you buy a bond,
you actually lend money to a company or government.
You get interest for this,
which is paid to you annually.

A bond usually costs around a thousand dollar.
Some bonds have a certain duration,
for example 10 years.
If this bond gives 5% interest,
with a duration time of 10 years.
And you buy this bond.

Then you get the upcoming 10 years,
50 dollar in interest each year.
After that 10 years, you get your deposit,
that thousand dollar back.

Some bonds have no duration in years mentioned.
There is a P mentioned, the abbreviation for Perpetual,
which means eternal.
These perpetual bonds pay interest annually, for eternity.
As long as the organization that issues them still exists.
That can be hundreds of years.

You buy a bond once,
and get 50 dollar in interest each year,
for the next 50 years or longer.
Without having to do anything else for it!

That's better, is it not?

Preparation

Before you start building your own Fortune,
we must do the preparation first.
The preparation consists of 3 things.

1. Have your will prepared by a notary.

This is not fun, but important.
So that when you're gone,
there are no ambiguities or misunderstandings.
About what you leave behind and to whom.

2. Make sure you are well insured.

Get the insurances that you need,
and think that you will need.
Such as a term life insurance policy and
a funeral insurance.
So that when you're gone,
your surviving relatives do not get stuck with those costs.
And still have to arrange things.
But that everything is already well arranged.

Try to get all your insurance policies from 1 or 2 providers, so that you get a discount on your insurance package.

3. Open the following 3 accounts:

1 A savings account,
2 a deposit account,
3 an investment account.

(Note : with deposit account is meant a bankingaccount on which you can fix an savingsamount of money,
for 1 to 20 years.
Which pays you interest annually,
and gives back your savingsamount,
after the duration period ends,
which you pick. If you want your savingsamount back before duration ends,
you get a fine.)

Systematically building it up

You will systematically on these 3 accounts,
build your Own Fortune.
With the amount of your income,
that you save every month.

If you, like in our previous example,
save per month 300 dollar.
Then you divide that 300 dollar,
about your 3 bankingaccounts.
1/3 Saving, so you put 100 dollar in your savings account.
1/3 Deposit, so you put 100 dollar in your deposit account.
1/3 Investing, so you put 100 dollar in your investment account.

Half of your investment account money, you invest in a
dividend yielding mutual fund.
And the other half you invest in an interest yielding bonds
mutual fund.

For example :

50 dollar in the NN Utilities Fund Dis
50 dollar in the Triodos Sustainable Bond Fund

You can leave it that way, all year round.
Without having to worry about it.

After that year, you will receive interest from your savings
account.
And interest from your deposit account.

And dividend & interest from your investment account.

This money works for you now.
That's how you let it grow.
You also get over the years,
the interest on interest effect.
Which makes it grow faster.

Every month

Next month you pay yourself first,
by saving 10% of your income.

This amount of 300 dollar you divide again over your 3 bankingaccounts.
1/3 Saving, so 100 dollar into your savings account.
1/3 Deposit, so 100 dollar into your deposit account.
1/3 Investing, so 100 dollar into your investment account.

Half of your investment account money,
you invest in a dividend yielding real estate mutual fund.
The other half you invest in an interest yielding bonds mutual fund.

For example :

50 dollar in the BNP High Income Property Fund
50 dollar in the NN Global Bond Fund

In total you have:

200 dollar in your Savings account.
200 dollar in your Deposit account.
200 dollar in your investment account
The money in your investment account is
equally divided over 4 mutual funds.

This means for you,
that you receive annual interest on your savings account.
And that you receive annual interest on your deposit account.
And that your receive annual dividend &
interest on your investment account.

Every year.

The next month you do the same 3 steps again
Step 1: You save 10% of your income.

Step 2: That 10%, in our example that 300 dollar, you divide over your 3 accounts.

A third into your savings account.
A third into your deposit account.
And a third into your investment account.

Step 3: The amount that goes into your investment account, you divide in two.
One half you invest in a dividend yielding mutual fund
or
a dividend yielding real estate mutual fund.
The other half you invest in an interest yielding bonds mutual fund.

The next month you do the same 3 steps again.

Then you do the same 3 steps each month.

Why not put everything in your investing account?

It is very important that you,

stick to the described dividing.
With this dividing you only risk
a third of your money.

But by having that part that you risk,
spread well.
You reduce the risk.

Mutual funds are already spread in themselves.
A mutual fund is invested in 50, 100 or more companies.

Which reduces your risk dramatically.

The amount with which you pay yourself first every month,
that 10% that you save.
Always divide it into your 3 accounts as below:
1/3 of that 10% in savingsaccount
1/3 of that 10% in depositaccount
1/3 of that 10% in investingaccount

It is wise to also, divide your investments in mutual funds
by category,
as below :

1/3 stocks mutual funds
1/3 bonds mutual funds
1/3 real estate mutual funds

Choose mutual funds that pay you dividends or interest.

It depends
It could be,
that your savings account pays the interest per month.
Or per year.
That differs per bank and savings account.

It could be that your mutual funds
pay out the dividend per quarter.
Or per year.
That differs per mutual fund.

If you open a deposit account at Rabobank,
the so-called Target Savings.
Then you can decide for yourself,
how often you put money into it,
and how much.
That is a very convenient deposit account.

It may be that other banks,
request a minimum deposit for a
deposit account.
For example 500 dollar.

If the bank where you open your deposit account,
requires a minimum deposit .
Then you can save that up monthly,
until you have enough to meet the minimum requirement and put
it in a deposit. For several years.

In our example,
you have after 5 months (5 x 100) =
500 dollar,
saved up.
You then meet the minimum requirement for a depositaccount.
And you can put 500 dollar in your depositaccount,
fixed for 10 years or more.

After 1 year

After 1 year you saved in total
3600 dollar.
(12 months x 300 = 3600 dollar)

You have done the 3 steps on a monthly basis.

Now you have:

1/3 of 3600 is 1200 dollar and that is in your savings account.
1/3 of 3600 is 1200 dollar and that is in your deposit account.
1/3 of 3600 is 1200 dollar and that is in your investment account.

You have spread your investments in mutual funds per category,
So :

1/3 of 1200 is 400 dollar and that is in stocks mutual funds.
1/3 of 1200 is 400 dollar euro and that is in bond mutual funds.
1/3 of 1200 is 400 dollar and that is in real estate mutual funds.

You have invested in mutual funds that
pay out dividend and
interest, to you.

So you receive interest and dividend on your investment account.
You will receive interest on your deposit account.
And you also receive interest on your savings account.

Step 4 and 5

Step 4: If you have 1200 dollar in mutual funds, you sell 1100 of it.

In our example, you have invested 1200 dollar every year in mutual funds.

So every year you sell 1100 dollar from your mutual funds.

So that you have 1100 dollar in cash, on your investment account.

Step 5: With that 1100 dollar cash on your investment account, you buy 1 individual bond.

A bond that pays a high interest rate to you, and has a long duration time.

Or a perpetual bond that pays a high interest to you.

**Note : It is forbidden for you to buy junk bonds !
Corporate and government bonds are allowed.**

Na 10 jaar

If you do the described steps,
every month and every year.
The next 10 years.

Then you will have :

1200 x 10 years = 12000 dollar on your savings account.
1200 x 10 years = 12000 dollar on your deposit account.
1200 x 10 years = 12000 dollar on your investing account.

Every time you had 1200 dollar
in mutual funds,
you sold 1100 dollars of it.
And from that cash you bought 1 bond.
So after 10 years you have 10 bonds.

If you have bought perpetual bonds,
that pay 10% interest per year,

You receive (10 x 100) = 1000 dollar in interest annually.

Well then you can buy 2 bonds per year.
From what you save and divide into your investingaccount
& from the interest payout from your bonds.

This will result in increasing your total annual receivable rturns.

Increasingly bigger annual returns for you

In the course of time, your total returns annually, increase by the interest & dividend that you receive.
This allows you to buy more and more bonds per year.
And thus, your total annual returns become even bigger.

For example after many years:

You have 10 perpetual bonds that pay 10% interest annually, you receive 1000 dollar per year in interest.
And you have 100 bonds that have a duration time of 20 years, which payout 8% interest.
You then receive 8000 dollar per year in interest.

Plus the interest that you receive on your savings account

& plus the interest that you receive on your deposit account.

In total, your annual returns are more than ten thousand dollars.

And with that you can buy more individual bonds, so that your total annual returns become even bigger.

In this way,
the system is reinforcing itself,
to yield bigger annual returns for you,
every year,
for the rest of your life.

What now & how do you proceed ?
If you understand this book,
and you understand all the steps
that you have to do.
If you are going to do everything yourself,
then that's fine.

Get started.

Start building your Fortune.

If you think you can use some help,
you can ask that someone.
You can ask your adviser at the bank.
Or you find an independent consultant.
Then you can together
Build your Fortune.

———————

Put this book in a place,
so that you see it every day.
So that it reminds you of your goal:

Building your own Fortune.

And so it reminds you of the steps you have to do every month
& every year.

———————————————

Thank you for buying this book

&

good luck with

Building Your Fortune.

P.S. I recommend that you reread this book every month. To stay focused.

If you like this book and get good value from it,
please be so kind to recommend it to the people that you know.

Or sent a copy or 2 as a gift.

So that it helps them to

improve their lives also.

Thank you.

Victory....

The bio of author Jasmin Hajro, nice to meet you Hello
dear reader, how are you ? Thank you for buying my book Victory .
My name is Jasmin Hajro, I was born on July 6, 1985 in Bosnia.
As refugees, we came to the Netherlands 21 years ago.
After having completed school & worked at several jobs ...
On 17 December 2012, I founded my first company: investment firm Jasko.
After a successful first year, I unfortunately had to close that company.
After a short period of rest, unemployment and temporary work.
I started again as an entrepreneur.

On September 1, 2015, I founded establishment Hajro.
(We say establishment instead of company, because we do a bit more then just sell stuff.
Like providing jobs, donating to 15 different charities, and helping people to live richer.)
Since the beginning the core activity is, selling sets of greeting cards, door to door.
Nowadays the product range has been expanded.
With, among other things, the selling of my more than 45 books.
Part of the royalties of my books are donated to the charity: foundation Giveth Life.
My company has a few different subsidiaries, like Hajro Franchise, Hajro Publishing
and Hajro International.
For more information about my company & the foundation, go to my website :
www.hajro-international.webnode.nl

Victory

Hello again... I am Jasmin Hajro, and you just have read a few things about me in my bio. But you have bought this book because you want to know the whole story. My life story .... I called it Victory, because I have overcome a few things. I am 32 years old and live in Doetinchem, in the Netherlands. I work as a salesman on behalf of Hajro. I sell sets of greeting cards, gift mugs and booklets. Part of the proceeds go to more than 15 Charities. You can find everything about establishment Hajro at
www.hajro.be (dutch company website)
or at www.hajro-intarnational.webnode.nl (english company website)

I now live in the Netherlands.
But on 6 July 1985 I was born in Sarajevo, in Bosnia. When I was a young child, we lived in Gora. That is a village in Bosnia. It is on a mountain. A mountain village. The view is great, lots of nature. Clean, fresh air. I remember it as a happy time. The house we lived in was a kind of 2 houses under 1 roof. Aunt Rahima had lived in the other part. Until her own house was built. My parents both worked, and I went to Biba, an elderly woman in the village, that was my babysitter. I remember she had an old-fashioned stove, which worked on firewood. And we placed unripe walnuts behind the stove, to ripe. Under our house, you had a steep part of soil, and below that a flat piece of land. On that flat piece of land, we grew vegetables, potatoes and very small tomatoes. There were also pear trees and walnut trees growing there. My mother worked at Tas, an automobile factory, where they made or processed. small car parts. I do not remember anymore what kind of work my father did then ... You notice that it has been a very long time ago. I was always very happy to see him, when he came home. And asked once if he could work 2 days a week, and be free 5 days a week. My uncle Ibro lived close to us, with Aunt Sevda and my nieces : Sanela and Amela. They had a red swing. I have

been swinging on it and went as high as possible, Until I got a kind of butterflies in my stomach feeling, by excitement. I do not know how to exactly describe that feeling. With my cousins I did play games such as hide & seek. I once wrestled with my father and then I ended up falling weird on my wrist, it hurted. Then Dad said: hajmo kod Ibre rostiljat Let's go barbequing at Uncle Ibro. I went to the mosque, and learned prayers and how to pray. I asked the hodza that's a kind of reverend, how you can know if someone is lying. He said you can see it on the forehead. That it turns a little red. It is very peaceful in the mosque, I still see it that way. Although it has been a while since I visited one.

_____

It is now March 27, 2018, 00:44 hours at night. I'm getting out of bed in the mornings, late again.... I wake up at 9 or 10 in the morning from the alarm clock. I then switch off the alarm. And fall asleep again. When I wake up again afterwards it is already noon. I had sleeping pills a few weeks ago, for 2 weeks.. It went well I started going to bed earlier, and getting up earlier. Before noon. Maybe it is a strange time, in the middle of the night to write a book. But I thought that once, I just had to start writing it. When I was playing at Chess Club Doetinchem, I said to Frans that I wanted to write a book about my life. That could have been in 2009. _____

Biba, the woman who looked after me when my parents worked, was also the babysitter of an orphan. I do not remember what his name was. But we went to the mosque together. There he farted ... And we were both thrown out. My father drove a Fico, that is like a kind of old model Fiat 500 car. If we drove to Grandpa and Grandma, I could sit on Dad lap behind the wheel. The first time I saw snow, I walked outside in my pajamas. I was completely stunned to look at it. Amazing. It must have been cold outside. The winters in Bosnia are colder than here. My father became very angry, and I got a beating with his belt. I remember that I was rolling over the ground and called: nemoj babo Don't hit me, Dad My index finger was completely swollen, because I was hit there too. I still love it to look outside when it snows. Everything seems so peaceful then. Oh, those beatings were normal. That was how you got punishment, and how other children received punishment in Bosnia. I was 6 years old when I went to school for the first time. When my sister, Emina was born and I saw her for the first time, she looked tinted. And I thought she was not my sister. My father once had in an angry mood, thrown the TV out of the window. I have around my twentieth year done the same thing once. Once my father went to Aunt Rahima, and I was not allowed to go with him. Then I went outside and looked in through the window at them. My father got angry, and I had to sit naked in front of the house. If I wanted a beating, then I could ask my daddy, he told me. My father drank, mom says he beat her too. The war had started between Bosnia and Serbia. We had moved because the enemies came too close. We have moved a number of times. My father had to fight for Bosnia, in the battlefield. And was not always with us. We left the village and we were in an abandoned house. I do not remember what that place is called. We have harvested grain, and grown potatoes. We took care of the cow of uncle Ibro, Galava. On my fathers request, I had tied Galava to a tree, so she could graze grass. But I hadn't shortened the chain and she had too much walking space so she had eaten a number of our potato plants. I got another beating. You could hear the shooting from a distance. A house near the one where we were in, was blown up. We left that place in the evening. A previous hotel became at that time a shelter for refugees. We spent a while there, and got food packages. I also fell on the stairs there with a bottle of milk, and had a cut on my wrist. It is been stitched and the scar looks like a cross. You can still see it, on my left hand.

My father was not with us in that shelter. I remember that we were waiting one time, with lots of people, probably for those foodpackets. It was so oppressive ...I felt like I was choking. My aunt Rahima had already fled to the Netherlands, and they arranged that we could go there too. I remember that I had to hold my sister's hand and was not allowed to let go. When we were with the cow walking through the forest. I do not know how long we have walked. My father stayed behind at a border. And said to mom prepare today for tomorrow & prepare tomorrow for the day after tomorrow We had help from a woman in Croatie. Eventually we were awaited somewhere by Aunt Rahima. We signed in as refugees. And went to an asylum seekers center, a period of time in Alkmaar .. And a period of time in Kampen near Dronten. There, I watched Lion King for the first time and almost had to cry, because I missed my father. We went to school and learned Dutch. After the asylum seekers' centers we got a Roahuis in Doetinchem, on the Leliestraat. (lilystreet) (a Roa house meant that we had a house and the government paid the costs for living, if I remember correctly) After 5 years we received the Dutch nationality. It was a red appartmentbuilding on the Leliestraat, where we lived. We got to know Zihra, who lived in the blue building. Also from Yugoslavia. There were 3 brothers in our red flat, a few houses further. One of them had hanged himself. My father came to the Netherlands wounded. We had those piggy banks, in which we saved money. So that dad could come to us. It would be like before, our family together ..... I played a fighting game with Dad on the Nintendo. And he made baked eggs in the morning. Very tasty. The reunification did not last long. My father left us. My parents then divorced. We got a rental house in Doetinchem, at the Ottawastreet 19.

_____

We are still living there now. Although mom now has a boyfriend, and is with him in the weekends. And my sister Emina, is now very pregnant. I will be an uncle, in a few weeks. I once already had described on paper this piece of my life : my time in Bosnia and the flight to the Netherlands. And called it Rebel. With more details, but I lost it. Or someone took it. After group 8 I went to the MAVO. At the Rietveld lyceum in Doetinchem. I obtained the Mavo diploma. The Mavo lasts 4 years, I think in the 3rd year of the Mavo, I had moved and lived with my father for a while. In Smilde, province of Drenthe. Then I came back to mom. Heartbroken. _____

I think this will become a series ...... Are you looking forward to the sequel? To be continued. Thank you for reading the first part of my life story.

prelude book Victory III

Hello Friend, how are you ? Is it weird that I call you friend? If you have bought and read Victory & Victory II, and you also bought Victory III, to read. Then you put so much trust in me, like a friend does. Thank you for being a loyal reader, I really appreciate it. I said that the proceeds (royalties) from my books go to the Giveth Life foundation, and that from there more than 40 other Charities receive donations. So, by buying this book, you now also support, more than 40 good causes. Thank you & congratulations. I should not actually do this ... But you have shown so much faith in me. It would be good then, to prove to you, that what I say, also really happens. So I trust you, that you deal confidentially with it, with that proof. Ok? You've seen a bank statement, from the account number of the Giveth Life Foundation. You see that my book revenue (royalties) have been paid out, by Kobo. And you see evidence, that every day donations are made to Charities, with modest amounts. And monthly with a larger amount. (stichting means foundation) The donations, that goes on every day & every month ... I set that up, that it goes automatically. Because I am the founder & treasurer from the Giveth Life foundation. And you are now a donor & support more than 40 Charities, because you bought this book. Wooohoooo

Together with you we support : Foundation Let the sick child enjoy, Mini manna foundation, Doctors without borders, Kika (children with cancer), West Achterhoek Library,Natural monuments 's Graveland Association, Save the children, AAP foundation, Cliniclowns, Achterhoek Animal Center, VIOD, Gasthuisfonds, Animalfate Foundation, Royal Dutch police dog association, Joni Foundation, Chess Association Doetinchem, NDD Swimming Association, Kidney Foundation, foundation Energy 4 all, Cordaid, foundation friends of the Slingeland hospital, foundation diva nearby, Kwf cancer control, foundation mama cash, Warchild, Chance fund, Lepra foundation, Refugeeswork Netherlands, Food bank Doetinchem, Doetinchem hockey club, Free press unlimited, Orange Fund, Animal Protection, Mother Teresa Foundation National MS fund, Noordbikers, Plan Nederland, Heart foundation, Scouting Netherlands Fund, Unicef, Light for the World, Terre des Hommes Foundation, Humanitas Association, Greenpeace Foundation, Cheer up Foundation, Children's Stamp Foundation, Tuberculosis Foundation, Baby Hope Foundation,UAF Foundation, Alzheimer's Foundation,

Parkinson's fund, Thomas relief fund Madras, World Wildlife Fund, Homeless people foundation, Rudolph foundation, V.V. Doetinchem, foundation Youth Sports Fund, Amnesty International, Bartimeus Sonneheerdt association & Handicapped sports in the Netherlands.

This is how we contribute together, to a better world. Together we can give more. Now you also understand why you can buy a paid version of book Recipe for Happiness. While you can also get the free version. Because the book is the same. You can give the paid version as a gift, while you also support more than 40 Charities. That way you get a feeling of fullfillment, by purchasing the paid version.

End of prelude.

book, the Great King

Secretly multiple atomic bombs were made…

But sir,
the people don't want war…

´ They are not for war…

For what are they then ?

To ensure peace,
the king said….

What shall we do about the riots and the rebellion ?

Continue with the 'Istina broadcast'
, the newspaper and the distribution of flyers….Everyday of the year

(Istina means truth in Bosnian language,
the king started his own television broadcasting station,
his own 'Istina' newspaper'
and the endless printing and delivery
of sales letters and marketing flyers….
Everyone in Bosnia gets mail from the king

Sadly …people don"t understand his policy,
he gets ridiculed like Donald Trump was on tv and internet
and people are rioting on the streets ,
to make matters worse : world leaders, kings and presidents of countries around the globe
are very nervous by his proposal, the NATO is threatening Bosnia with huge sanctions)

Proce…

said the king in Bosnian, it means
´it will pass´

He is a madman
the prime minister of England shouts…

in the presence of the Queen of england and her officials….

After he won the elections,
he reformed Bosnia
to a kingdom
and crowned himself as the king
putting other officials on the sidelines

with his so called board of advisors

He sends mail to every human being in Bosnia

and he started his own tv broadcasting station
and owns a newspaper

it´s all very convenient for his propaganda…

Do you realize that he has tore down buildings
that were businesses in operation
and put the people in jail ?

I see, replied the queen….calmly

Madam, he has enough arms to destroy countries, perhaps the whole world,
his proposal is an act of war !

With her decades of experience in ruling a country of world power
she calmly replies : I have sent people of the Royal Guard to investigate
what is really happening…

We shall wait
until we have the facts….

Constitution of kingdom Bosnia

Law 1 : every resident of Bosnia is free to choose his education, work and religion…

Law 2: every resident of Bosnia has the right to a sufficient income, if he works and when he doesn´t work….

Law 2b : the minimum wage in the kingdom of Bosnia is 2000 KM or 1000 euros a month.

Law 3: every resident of Bosnia has the right to a sufficient pension, from the age of 65, the monthly minimum amount is 2000 KM or 1000 euros.

Law 4: it is forbidden for the Bsonian army to attack any country in the world, the Bosnian army is only allowed by law to defend it´s own country…

Law 5 : every resident of kingdom Bosnia has life insurance and health insurance including dental, the health insurance premiums are paid for by the government…

Law 6 : Everyone in Bosnia must pay 50% taxes

Law 6b : corporations unable to pay the 50% tax get subsidy,
people unable to pay the 50% tax get subsidy

Law 7 : salesmanship and entrepreneurship are highly encouraged and subsidized.

Law 8 : all in need of an income or pension, will be accepted by the ´Agencija´ offices of which there are 1000 offices in the country

Law 9 : essential skills as cooking, personal finance, saving and investing, running a household, running a business, are taught at school and are mandatory

Law 10 : every resident of kingdom Bosnia when reaching the age of 18, must serve for 1 year in the army to learn discipline

Mister president,
what do we do ?

What does the satellite footage show ?

A few riots….
the rich people of Bosnia are angry

Why is that ? asked the president…

Well, because they have to pay 50% in taxes.

Really ?

Yes sir

And everyone´s debt has been erased

Really ?

Yes sir

Is he really training everyone to be a soldier ?

Everyone who reaches the age of 18, has to serve 1 year in the army…
It´s mandatory by Law.

What are the current military operations of them ?

All the soldiers are in Bosnia,
every base is staffed,
but with less people…
The rest is gardening.

Gardening ???

Yes sir….
they are building natural parks , all across the country

That is what the footage shows,
it is also on many news broadcasts
around the world…

And it is forbidden ….by law...for the Bosnian army to invade any country ?

It is Bosnian law sir, it is part of their Constitution.
The king has obviously not always been
a king…

He was not even a real politician…

Most years of his life he has been a business man,
and he wrote a lot of books….

He has even videos on Youtube…

´´Znate da se nije bilo posla, para ,penzija i hrane ,
posle rata…
Sad po zakonu, svako ima
primanje, para, hranu, kucu, slobodu´´
´Śvako ima zdravljeno osiguranje…
Vazno je ,narode moj, da svako ima…
Eh, da svako ima , svi placamo malo vise poreza.
Puno vam hvala za vase
povjerenje u mene, u vladu i nasu drzavu´´

What did he say ?

You all know that there was no work, money, pensions and food
after the war…
Now, by Law, everyone in Bosnia
has a income, money, food , a house, freedom´´
Everyone has health insurance…
It is very important that everyone (every resident of Bosnia)
my people,
that everyone has these things…
For every resident of kingdom Bosnia, to have these things,
we all pay a bit more taxes…
I thank you for your faith in me,
our government and our country.

In a big castle
in beautiful Bosnia
the meeting began…
World leaders attended,
they ones who had agreed to visit the king of Bosnia ….

Sir, thank you for your proposal for a everlasting peace,
and the opportunity to do business
by import and export
We do have some questions…

Thank you all for visiting
the king said,
pushing his meal from the McDonalds aside...

You say, all you do is for the good of your country and your people,

Yes.

Then why are they rioting against you ?

Besides every moque I have built a church and a synagoge
and a room for Eastern religions…
Not everyone likes that…

When they refused, you have torn down buildings!

I think...
the religious people should not only preach peace and tolerance
they should practice it…
said the king, in his powerful heavy voice…

The rich people in Bosnia are angry because they dislike the rate of taxes…
50% is a lot
For years they have avoided and evaded paying taxes
Now they must pay or they go to jail
until it is paid

The religious people are angry because they have to pay taxes
for the first time in their life,
and they particularly hate that half of their possessions
mostly gold
has been sanitized….

What ?

That is unheard of ….

So you take their gold
to put in your royal treasure chests ?
the chanselor asked suspiciously..

The gold has been melted and sold,
the proceeds went into
rebuilding peoples houses
and after that was done
it went into
restoring buildings and roads…

I see, said the queen of England…

Mister Cenga,
you keep the postal offices busy…

people say that is how you share your propaganda….

The New Bosnian Constitution
is delivered to every resident of Bosnia
as are the other laws,
financial statements,
and other news concerning the changes
in law and government
So that my people can see, how the money that they pay in taxes
is used….

How much does the royal family of Bosnia get ?

They get minimum wage

I see, said the chanselor of Germany

Which has doubled several times, you mean….

The king replied : It is the new standard, the new minimum wage,
it is meant to be sufficient to live,
enough to pay your bills, with enough money to save and invest
and to enjoy life

We can not ignore all the news reports about the politicians in your country

While they talk

the ferocious bloodsuckers…..
I mean politicians……….(the king smiled)
while they talk and congregate
I get work done…
said the king.

I still don´t know what to think about gardening soldiers….
Is that just a facade, while you are getting ready for war ?

It is very therapeutic for them...my soldiers….
and it restores nature in overbuilt cities...
we are ahead of schedule for our climate change goals and requirements
the electric cars are getting more mainstream
the subsidy helps progress

Gardening companies pay the soldiers who are gardening,
it saves Bosnian government billions a year…
Part of this money went into restoration
of buildings, roads
of everything that was destroyed in the war

A part goes into health and life insurance for the residents of Bosnia

A part goes into subsidy for salespeople, and entrepreneurs and business owners…

A healthy positive surplus remains….

Every quarter there is a celebration and parade of the season….

And still plenty of money remains available….

Bosnia has withdrawn all charitable and humanitarian donations…

Yes, replied the king..
We first had to solve our own problems

Excuse me
said the king
as he stood up
´My sister will take over from me
thank you all´
and he slowly left the room

We have more questions for your brother
they said…

My brother needs to rest
he has been shot,
luckily he survived

The princess took a moment
to regain her emotions
and continued …

Our country is prosperous and thriving
after a short period of time
More than 100 countries have accepted
our peace proposal
and are doing business with Bosnia
including Russia, China and Turkey
My brother has received many presents from world leaders around the globe

The queen of England smiled to the young Bosnian princess….

I hope you liked my story
Please share my work with friends, family and booklovers.

For more information and to find my other books
please visit me at www.jasminhajro.com

Hi dear reader, how are you ? I am Jasmin Hajro, and you just have read a few things in my bio about me. But you have bought this book because you want to know the whole story. My life story .... I called it Victory, because I have overcome a few things. So, I am Victorious. And you as a donor of more than 40 charities are Victorious too. Did you enjoy Victory ? Sorry for the spelling mistake in it. Welcome to Victory II I am 32 years old and live in Doetinchem, in the Netherlands. I work as a salesman on behalf of Hajro. I sell sets of greeting cards, gift mugs and booklets. Part of the proceeds go to Charities. You can find everything about it at www.hajrobv.nl It's now March 31, 2018, 23:52 hours. On this Saturday I am free .... Well, I have prepared the presents for customers today, and also the business cards and mugs. For next week. I bought some groceries, vacuumed the house. And have eaten 3 times. Then I went for a run. It was half past 10 in the evening. It also started to rain and I was soaking wet after my jogging lap. Then I smoked some tabacco and drank a cup of tea. But do not tell anyone. Yes, I smoke tabacco, and I jog. There are no excuses for not exercising. If a smoker can do it, then you can certainly do it too. After showering, I ate my midnight snack. A piece or 6 sandwiches with cheese and a glass of milk. My sister and her husband have returned from a wedding and have went to bed. Beamy our cat, also came home.

Maybe you think that I've written and published , a lot of books in a short period of time .... That is not a mystery. First of all, my books are short. I believe you do not need to write an encyclopaedia, to teach someone something. We used to have an offer at the Hajro E-store, the VIP. That is a luxury greeting card subscription, where you get all kinds of extra bonuses. The Recipe for Happiness would be included for free. And it would be about one page long. But it is now a comprehensive valuable guide, and become a nice book. You know the period when there were so many people fired at the banks ... I then got a good idea By means of a program, the bank could help people to become rich and instead of firing employees, keep them and hire new staff. Tired and feverish, I had neatly typed out my program. And I went to ING bank with it. They did not want it. And that program became my book the lifebuoy for banks " loyal banking " As you can see, the book was basically ready.

I have many years ago written a number of poems . It has also been years since I had been sending messages and jokes via Facebook to Rietje. (A girl I fell in love with, who had been a coworker) I had printed out all those messages and put them in a folder. So my book Poems, jokes and book, was also largely finished. If I ask you to describe me how your day was today ... That would not be that difficult for you. If I asked you to describe how your past month was. Then that too, would not be difficult for you. So for my book Victory, it was a matter of sitting down rolling up my sleeves and starting to write. I just described how my life has been in that period of time. So, therefore, Well, you now know how I , in short chunk of time, have been able to write & publish a number of books. Ok, that being said, where were we ? When I did the MAVO education (general secondary education If I translate correctly), I had lived with my father for a while. And returned heartbroken to mommy. It had hurt me a lot, when my father left us. When we lived in Lilystreet (Leliestraat)We had missed him for so long, and had those piggy banks in which we saved money, so that dad could come to us. From Bosnia. And after being reunited for such a short time, he left us. Maybe then as a child I thought, that he did not want us, and that he did not want me. So he went to live in Smilde, we stayed in Doetinchem. I missed him very much, and wanted to live with him. My mother had a boyfriend at the time who then drove me to dad, I believe. My father had a new wife, she is Dutch, and has 2 daughters from her previous marriage. I went to the Nassau college there, in Assen. I had to every morning travel for 1 hour on my bicycle to get to school.

I especially liked going to my aunt Kasema , and spending time with my cousins. Aunt Kasema is Papa's younger sister. She has 2 sons and 1 daughter. We played super mario on a game computer. And had lots of fun. At school things were going ok. I could hardly share my father at home with them. In principle, we were nice to each other. I started my puberty then, I think. I was pulled back and quiet. I listened to rap music. At school I was friends with Robert, who called himself Skip. In the break we were once driving around on his scooter. I was on the back seat. A bit driving through the city, and in front of the police station, without helmets on. Then we slipped and fell down while taking a curve. My father was not happy. This is how the tensions built up at home .. In the end I could choose either change my behavior or return to my mother. So I went back to mom, sad. I went through the 4th class of the Mavo at the Ludger college. I then started to smoke. Cigarettes. To try what it was like. The first time I became dizzy. Then it became a habit. Then I started to smoke weed. To try it. I never liked the smell. It was funny at first, with periods of time in which I started laughing at almost anything. Then that became a habit. And it seemed like I was less active. I had been practising karate for more than a year. I was stoned every weekend. Watching movies, eating chips. Hanging around. I became friends with Kai, a classmate. We had fun. We got one time a block of hash, to sell. We eventually ended up smoking the whole thing ourselves. We have that movie, Pulp Fiction seen about 20 times. Very very stoned. Just so often, that we had memorized the dialogues from the film. Like :

Ezekiel 25:17 the path of the righteous man is beset on all sides by the inequities of the selfish and the tyranny of evil men Blessed is he who in the name of charity and goodwill Shepherds the weak through the valley of darkness And I will strike down upon thee with great vengeance and furious anger Those who attempt to poison and destroy my brothers And you will know that my name is the lord When I lay may vengeance upon thee....

I even now remember the lines. Ridiculous right ? Maybe we have seen that movie 30 times. Later I started to experiment with other drugs. Xtc tablets and speed. Of course I had tasted my very first beer, a while ago. So I often drank beer and smoked weed to become strunk. Stoned and drunk. At the same time. I went way over my limits, and had to vomit quite some times because of too much booze. I started to go higher more often with those pills. When taking them, you feel really good, you gett energy from them, and I went to drink a lot of coffee so that the effect lasted longer. Eventually I was awake all night after taking 5 pills, and just continued to take even more. We sat in a park with some people who I did not know. Me and Pino. That's what everyone called him. I also sniffed some speed and drank red vodka. At a given moment, we started walking home. And was it was like I could see the wind. I had taken 10 or 15 tablets. I began to hyperventilate. When we arrived at home it was already morning ... I was looking very pale, and wanted to drink water but couldn't. I walked back and forth, could not stop. I thought my chest would explode. In a hallucination, I saw a big black hole, thought I was going to die and peed in my pants. My mother and sister had come down and panicked. I think someone called the police and I was thrown into a van. Then the lights went out, I lost consciousness. I woke up in a hospital bed. My father came and asked if I knew what I looked like. I said no. My face was swollen. I had been in a coma for several hours. They had said to my mother: if he does not wake up, then he will not survive. This happened in a point of time in my life ,when I was working in the hospitality industry , at restaurant the Mirror (de Spieghel). Pretty quickly after my neardeath experience, I went back to work again. I came to work a few times too late and was fired there.

I have tried the Havo education, (higher general secondary education) the adult education program, but that did not work out. I registered at temporary employment agencies and worked at jobs that they offered me. Mainly productionwork. I have after that coma, once tried to smoke a joint. I didn't feel good, got palpitations. That was the last time. From then on, I stopped taking drugs. I did still drink alcohol. And now also whiskey. It often went with those jobs the same way.. I did it for a while. I worked, earned. Started to show up late. And was fired or did not show up anymore. I applied for a job in 2007 at Palestra / Landal, and started working as a dishwasher. I came too late there, too though I did not have to start working until the afternoon. There was a positive atmosphere, and we always had a drink after work with coworkers. Once I got at home, I kept on drinking. I was allowed to help on the cold side of the kitchen, to prepare appetizers and desserts. After some time, I was fulltime on the cold side. Eventually I also learned the warm side of the kitchen, making soups. Baking fish and steak. Cooking lunch and dinner. I worked hard, I wanted to live better. One day after my birthday, after I had drunk a lot. I collapsed and fell to the floor. (Perhaps becaue of too much drinking and fatigue) I then stopped drinking alcohol. I had a permanent job there. The work became hard to do, until I didn't funtion there at all anymore. I got resigned. Fired.

Then I was at home and had the feeling that I broke down. I received a unemployment benefit. In the last years that I had worked there, I started watching motivating videos on youtube. From Jim Rohn and Brian Tracy. I also received a journal as a gift, an empty book to write in. While working at Landal, I earned well and had few expenses. I saved and did a home study course : Wiser with money. Then I learned to invest myself. By taking another home study course, read books about investing and by investing myself. Somewhere I read about pensions and the pension discount. If you have worked abroad for a number of years or are a immigrant and have not 67 years of employment history, then you get less pension. My parents would then receive a half-pension, they had a big problem. I wanted to get rich ever since. So that I could give them a good pension.

I have read books about becoming rich. Listened to audiobooks. Eventually, I came up with a financial system. To systematically build up a fortune. I have applied for a patent. And I described the system in my first book: How you build your own fortune with simple steps. I have now published the 3rd edition of that book, with the title Build your Fortune. (I have received a patent on February 27th 2018.) I could not find a job after that unemployment benefit. I have emailed many job applications. A lot employment agencies I visited. In person I had visited with my resume, more than 100 companies . They did not have a job for me. What could I do? I did not want to go back to the hospitality industry anymore. I liked investing a lot more. So I started my first company called Jasko, on December 17, 2012 An investment company. The saving and investing that I did for myself, I could also do for other people. I have had a relationship, a number of times with a girl. I fucked Hilde for the first time when I was 16. Later I also have had sex with a girlfriend of my mother . Which is like 20 years older than me.

To be continued.
Are you looking forward to the sequel ?
It will be released on July 6th 2022

"Note by november 22, 2020,
''You can read it on the following pages''

book Victory III

Hello Friend, how are you ? Is it strange that I say friend to you? If you have bought and read Victory & Victory II, and you also bought Victory III, to read. Then you put so much faith in me as a friend does. Thank you for being a loyal reader, I really appreciate it. I said the revenues (royalties) from my books to the Giveth Life foundation, and that from there more than 40 other Charities receive donations. So, by buying this book, you now support them too, more than 40 Charities. Thanks & congratulations. I really shouldn't be doing this … But you have so much faith in me I can show you. It would be fine then to prove to you, what I say also happens. So I trust you that you treat it confidentially, with that piece of evidence. Ok? You've seen a bank statement now of the Giveth Life Foundation account number. You see my book revenue (royalties) paid out there on, by Kobo. And you see evidence that every day is donated to Charities, with modest amounts. And monthly with a larger amount. The donations, that goes on every day & every month ... I set it up like this that it is automatic. Because I am the founder & treasurer of the Giveth Life foundation. And you are now a donor & supports more than 40 charities, because you bought this book. Wooohooo.

Together with you we support: foundation Let the sick child enjoy, foundation Mini manna, Doctors without borders, Kika, West Achterhoek Library, Association of nature monuments' s graveland, Save the children, AAP foundation, Cliniclowns, Achterhoek animal center, VIOD, Gasthuisfonds, Dierenlot foundation, Royal Dutch Police Dog Association, Joni Foundation, Chess Association doeinchem, NDD swimming club, Kidney Foundation, Energy 4 all foundation, Cordaid, friends of the Slingeland hospital foundation, foundation diva nearby, Kwf cancer prevention, foundation mama cash, War Child, Chance Fund, Leprosy Foundation, Dutch Council for Refugees, Food bank Doetincheem, Doetinchem hockey club, Free press unlimited Orange Fund, Animal Protection, Mother Teresa Foundation National MS fund, Noordbikers, Plan Nederland, Hartstichting, Scouting the Netherlands fund, Unicef, Light for the world, Terre des hommes foundation, Humanitas Association, Greenpeace Foundation, Opkikker Foundation, Children's Stamps Foundation, Tuberculosis Fund, Baby Hope Foundation, UAF Foundation, Alzheimer Foundation, Parkinson Fund, Thomas Aid Fund Madras, World Wildlife Fund, Street People Foundation, Rudolph Foundation, V.V. Doetinchem, Youth Sports Fund Foundation Amnesty International, Bartimeus Sonneheerdt association & Disabled sports in the Netherlands.

This is how we contribute together, to a better world. Together we can give more. Well maybe now you understand why you can purchase book Recipe for Happiness . While you can also read it for free. While it is the same book. You can give the paid version as a gift, but you also support more than 40 charities with it. That's how you get a smug feeling, by purchasing the paid version. Ok, where did left of ? So I would give the book Victory III to you ..... It will be about the past year, So 2018. And it should have some victories in it to honor the title. What victories….. I made an Eshop for the Giveth Life foundation you can visit it at: https://eshopstichtinggivethlife.jimdofree.com

I have done something different for once, I made a video book. Yes. So a video in which I am on reading my 3rd book Recipe for Happiness to you. Grab a nice cup of coffee or tea, sit or lie down comfortably and just play. You can find video book at: http://www.youtube.com

bottom left. I also made a Hajro Group Photo Book. I also made a Calendar for 2019, you can also order them there. (By now , 28 october 2020, Lulu has changed the author pages, but you can still view my videobook at www.youtube.com

I also made an author page on Goodreads. You can see it on:
https://www.goodreads.com/author/show/17686005.Jasmin_Hajro

I have also made some videos and put them on my author page at Amazon. You can see them on:
https://www.amazon.com/Jasmin-Hajro/e/B075GZPT4V

I've read some books of course, because I want to get better at selling.
And I recommend them to you too. They are :

Power of Self Confidence - Brian Tracy
Power of charm - Brian Tracy
21 great ways to become a sales superstar - B. Tracy
Stronger than ever - R. v / d Wolk
The secret of 100,000 - a year - L. Babeliowsky

I have also written and published some books, and made some bundles (boxsets). And my ebooks can also be ordered as paperback.
book Website www.hajrobv.nl in a booklet
book the Lifebuoy for banks``loyal banking " (paperback)
book the Ultimate Winning Strategy for Entrepreneurs (ebook)
book Poems, jokes and book (paperback)
book Victory I.
book Victory II
book Always work & always money in your pocket, every day.

I have made a new edition of the book Double your profits. (Double your Profits extended) Book Things You Don't Want to Know (I gave a copy of this to my dad for his birthday. Hopefully he can laugh about it)
book For you
My 14th book: starting your own business & making it successful, in the harsh reality where nobody cares.
Bundle The largest, best & most spectacular book in the world
Bundle or box set Double your profit & your bank balance in 4 months.
The bundles are collections of books .... In Double your profit & your bank balance in 4 months you get 5 books. (The bundle does consist of 3 parts)

And bundle The grand, best & most spectacular book in the world is 11 books in 1.
That's a bargain right ... You will then receive the entire Victorious series
My first series of books is that. Thank you God for all the good things in my life. I hope you don't mind that I just said a prayer of thanks. I am now writing the 3rd book of my SECOND series ... (series Work to Shine) I can be very grateful. Thank you too for reading my writing. And yes it is 2:30 in the morning. My little sister, the owner of Energie Nu & the princess of which I am uncle (her daughter) and her husband are still on vacation. They will come back in 1 week. My mother is still in a relationship with Peter, and I am very happy for her that she has found a good person. And I ? Tjah still single. First my life even better on track, after that I'll find a wife. Although I had the feeling a while ago that I was dying. It is a good & productive year after all... We should be grateful. Remember I would prove to you that together we support many charities? Here it comes..… Some names and numbers have been left out, for privacy. I hope you can read it ... Otherwise you can still view it at: https://www.hajrobv.nl/doen-wat-je-zegt-of-schrijf

And what about that patent? I have described that financial system in my book How to Build Your Own Fortune with Simple Steps (2nd edition) & in the 3rd edition, namely book Build your Fortune. I really recommend that you buy that book, and take the steps contained in it. Am I our 'hero'? I don't know if I did anything heroic. But I did do something spectacular maybe it is Legendary .... The following : One of the goals of company Hajro is doing something back for the Netherlands. Because the founder of Hajro (also called Jasko) is an immigrant & was well received in the Netherlands by the Dutch. Because his book Build your Fortune (what every household should have) is available free of charge to everyone in the Netherlands. To build a fortune or a good pension. Hajro Achieved This Goal! You can also read that on my homepage: www.hajrobv.nl

I have achieved one of my Long-term Goals. Great huh? I'm very happy. As you can see it's almost 3 in the morning when I wake up & get up in the morning in the morning may it be called a miracle. So I still struggle a bit with getting up early. After this I also have to publish this book, so it will be later. I still smoke too much black tabacco & drink more coffee than is good for me. But yes, you gotta die from something right ?. A week on the road with me (in short) I have from Sunday September 2, 2018 to Saturday, September 15 worked every day. Every day I started selling door to door for a long time. With sets of greeting cards & gift mugs. And I have found 47 customers times 5 euros that is 235 euros in turnover. I bought a birthday present for my sister. I gave my nephew a Quest magazine as a gift. (who lives in Assen) I paid my deliverer the fee. I bought Mary Kay hand cream as a gift for my mom. That Sunday after those 2 weeks, I was tired but satisfied. I then rested & watched movies. I had worked in city Doetinchem and on Sunday in town Didam.

Another victory I made 103 sales in September, my new record. (meaning I found 103 customers) That is 515 euros in turnover, plus 37, - in royalties of book sales. I'm lucky to still live with my mother. But I'm already halfway there. When I make 200 sales per month, I can basically look for a house. My mother is a person of gold. I'm going to earn a ton (100,000 euros) and then again. Then I will buy a house for my mom and a car (a purple one) Are you also going to do something spectacular for your parents? They are always there for you I hope you enjoyed and that I have kept my word on what I promised.

Victory IV

For my mother Azema Halilovic ... Thank you draga majko (dear mother) that you are always there for me. And that you gave me the time to build my company & to write so many books

Victory IV

Hey Hello how are you doing ? In principle, I'm fine ... yet it is a bit mixed ... it is Monday, April 20, 2020. it's been 2 months Corona time .. just a fucking flu .. old people with poor resistance die from the flu. Our neighbor has passed away, he had bad lungs for years. I worked anyway ... all this time… It's harder ... it takes much longer to find a customer and I face more closed doors. I found 3 today, 3 customers ... who have bought a set of our unique greeting cards … I designed them myself and only we have them, so they are unique. ''Note at the time of translation, Sunday november 22, I am human too, I could be wrong'' We have a temporary promotion ... or offer… the well known buy one, get one free... if you buy a set of greeting cards, then you get a giftmug for free. To cheer the people up a bit, in this "strange time" ". Maybe you got on the news that some businesses and shops are closed, there was talk of lockdowns of countries, they want people to keep their distance from each other and in the supermarket the cashier was wearing gloves. The paper said that if you didn't have any symptoms of a cold for 24 hours, you just got over it and you are fine... I have written 2 booklets in recent times ... For Saartje and Secrets of writing and selling books.

Due to current government measures I did get a Tozo ... which is corona crisis subsidy... Hoeray finally financial support from the government .. the money is of course nice, but above all it is the principle ... It means... we do not pay taxes for nothing. Because if you need help, you will get it ... apparently .. even if it just took a long time for me to get some. And only after my 6th application for benefits, the Tozo subsidy got approved. Dutch government and tax authorities ... Thank you. I don't feel like a 2nd class citizen anymore. With more than 36 books and still no bestseller ... I start to wonder if I am doing something wrong? What do you think ? But I know what it is ... Marketing ... I have to do more marketing ... maybe several thousand people know that I write books and where you can buy my books ... In a world of more than 6 billion people ....a several thousand is not so much people... I also write in my diary ... my journal ... a little less than I used to do lately ... I was busy... so I wrote those 2 books ... I have worked.. selling our greeting cards ...

I also made Author Merchandise ....maybe you think that's cool or nice .. Tshirt with "Victorious" on it or "Work to shine" like my book series ... and ofcourse also "" You legend " and an author mug And a Tshirt with a funny but true text: " My poo is black from all the coffee. I am a writer " Wouldn't it be funny to walk around with that ... In addition, also a Tshirt with the logo from my company Hajro and a sweater which is also printed with our logo. You can see them all at www. gumroad.com/jasminhajro I have made and delivered mix sets to our Member, a customer of mine who has a greeting card subscription, every month she receives greeting cards with something extra. And I also have working links put on my Author website, if you click on it then you actually end up on the website of the bookstores where my books are for sale. It all takes time to do and create and energy .. Maybe that's why I was a little tired the past few days.. I hadn't even thought about it ... And I also added Marketing for Author as a service to my company's services. Because that's what I and other book authors need. what I do for myself I can also do as a business for other people. Beethoven plays in the background while I write ... I like classical music ...

''Note by the time of translation, november 22nd 2020, my company's website is www.hajro.be
 I have paid for it a year upfront….so it's always online and working… I have a new Author website...whaich has a longass domain name…..but it's free and always online, avilable for you to visit and ofcourse online 24/7…..I give away 10 of my books on it….so it's worth a visit…..just remember the longass domain name which is www.jasminhajro6.webnode.nl '' This is one of the unique greetingcards, which is in a package of 5 greetingcards and envelopes, that I sell. (I have sold more than 700 of these packages of greetingcards) And this is the giftmug, full of candy that people get along with the package of greetingcards for free, for a limited time The mug has my company's logo printed on it and it also says : ''Enjoy life'' I was thinking of writing a fiction book a kind of "rant" " swearing on things I hate or to blow off steam ... as to "pickers" or pluckers... " too lazy to work want something for free ... living of other people by theft ... drug other people to pick them better ... What do you think ? Is it gonna be a weird fucking book? Should I just stay in my arena ... my box the NONfiction area…. I respect working people ... I like to work .. working has positively changed my life ... I know how hard some people have to work for their money ... I respect that ...

I jogged this afternoon ... it was going slow ... it has been a while since my last run... 1 or maybe 2 weeks ago that I was last running .. scandalous I know… I jogged a lot more in the past year ... I have to get back into the habit of running regularly. Sometimes I would like it to come back to someone at home after work… I'm alone for a long time .. I just haven't actively looked for a relationship ... I first wanted to get my life in order ... It's more or less in order ... I do not drink I don't use .. I don't make any problems .. I work… Ready? Ready for a relationship? First I'll have to earn a normal ... minimum of E 1500, - per month. Then at least I can do nice things with my woman.. .. good food and stuff and go to the McDonalds of course ... But also because it gives peace, when everything is paid. ''Another note, by the time of translation …. I know it's short… I don't like that either… I don't want to disappoint you…. It's just that I've been so busy.. building my business… designing new greetingcards…. Adding new products and services… and then I had to create a new company website and also a new author website… And when the corona crisis began… I had to do something to keep my business going… like the promotion… buy one, get one free…

I had to Apply for subsidy and funding… Then I decided that the best way to get through the crisis was.. to just keep on working… so I kept on selling door to door my greetingcards.. and I wrote more books… Sometimes I worked 6 or 7 days a week… and on my free day I would visit my sister and her kids… the girl is 2 years old now and the boy is 1 year old and he just started to walk... Here they are… my books of this crisis year… Through the crisis english Running out of time In loving memory Actie als strategie Rahima & Idriz Exposium Hajro, story & catalogus My story english Word miljonair in sales Wat het beste werkt ? na 7 jaar ondernemen Ondernemen met hersenschadE Productiviteit crash course And I also translated Victory 3 into english… and now also Victory 4… By november I got like exhausted… and took 3 to 4 days off every week…. And… well guess what..? I also wrote ''My little masterpiece'' I recommend you get that one.. the booklet has a great quote for everyday of the month.. they are things you can do… and they are lifechanging… for sale at : My little masterpiece (www.lulu.com

 And after that I wrote : I don't feel like writing, says the author it's more of a whitepaper… but it's still valuable… for sale at : I don't feel like writing says the author (lulu.com) These 2 booklets I have written in english it saves me the time of translating them… On the following pages you can read my booklets… the Recipe for Happiness and Overcoming tough times… or if you have already read them.. you can reread them… and find something of value … that you didn't see the first time…

Victory 5

Hello, how are you doing ? Thank you for choosing one of my books to read... Have you read Victory 1, 2, 3, and 4 ? Let's start with last year… 2020 corona time… I just kept on working all year long… I have been selling packages of greetingcards… for 52 weeks ,last year… I earned about E 5850,- euros I wrote new books and booklets… I wrote : Through the crisis Running out of time In loving memory Actie als strategie Rahima & Idriz Exposium Hajro, story & catalogus My story Word miljonair in sales Wat het beste werkt ? na 7 jaar ondernemen Ondernemen met hersenschadE Productiviteit crash course And the booklet : My little masterpiece and I kept on writing, the other titles I wrote are :
Victory 4
I don't feel like writing, says the author ,
Hackers are scouts ,
Being real and true: in times of fake and pretend ,
100 % sales rule,
200 % sales rule ,
3,
Entrepreneurship cursus ,
Quotes for success

I also made my author website at www.jasminhajro6.webnode.nl

And I made an international english website for my company Hajro at
www.hajrointernational.webnode.nl

It was a busy year, at the end of 2020 I slept for 3 days….. exhausted… I was disappointed that I hadn't earned more after working that hard….. but then I figured out why… I was just working half days… selling about 3 or 4 hours a day If you work half the time, you get half the pay half the money isn't enough… So My goal is to work more hours, selling door to door... At the beginning of 2021 I translated 3 of my dutch books into english, they are :
Tits, how do I write a book ?,
How to overcome my addiction ?,
Start your own business & make it successful. In the harsh reality, where nobody cares

My medication against hallucinations is working, it still sometimes happens very briefly.. My medications for sleeping also works, I sleep at 12 or 1 oçlock at night… I decided to be free on Sunday… In the past I would sometimes also go out selling on Sunday.. But now it's a mandatory free day My body and mind need to rest. I go for a run about once a week, I used to do it more often, I have to get back into the habit of doing it more often. I got a subsidy for 3 years, of E 650 euros a month which is settled with the earnings of my company.. If I earn 400 euros, I get 250 euro in subidy And I got help with my debts, I am in a program and have a budget coaching session every month and 3 years from now, in 2024 I will be finally debtfree That is my victory…

And becuse of the subsidy I don't need to worry about money.. another victory I have more peace of mind and I gained 4 kg I have visited my sister and her kids almost every Sunday… Last Friday I worked about 3 hours and sold 14 packages of greetingcards, earning E 70,- euros That's the 2nd or 3rd time that that happened… I watched a lot of South Park episodes and it was fun… After that I changed from watching entertainment to watching other videos about entrepreneurship, like the channel Valuetainment on youtube… And recently I have been watching the videos on the channel Coffeezilla, about all kinds of scammers… It seems there is a whole industry of people scamming people From worthless investments to overpriced courses and actors as business owners… It's offcourse pathetic for the people that are getting scammed a shame especially if they loose their lifes savings… Those people make it harder for real entrepreneurs and salespeople, because they make people untrusting…. The only thing I can do is to not make unrealistic claims., offer a 3 month money back guarantee and be open and transparant, with my company and my books.. I am also on the waiting list for a assisted or guided living.. So within a year or so I will be living on my own, leaving my mothers house.. I think I can do it, I can prepare a meal.. I am sorry, that it's short… but that sums up last year I have added more books to this one, they are : Last 10 years,
Build your Fortune,
Overcoming tough times the,
Ultimate Winning Strategy,
and Recipe for Happiness

You can buy Victory 5 and gets all those books also in the box set
or books bundle which is book Victory 5,
I have added more books to it,
to give more value to my readers and fans.

Kind regards, Jasmin Hajro

To read more books by Jasmin Hajro, please go to www.jasminhajro.com
or www.lulu.com/spotlight/jasminhajro

Victory 5

The bio of entrepreneur & author Jasmin Hajro, nice to meet you Hello dear reader, how are you ? Thank you for buying my booklet ... My name is Jasmin Hajro, I was born on July 6, 1985 in Bosnia. As refugees, we came to the Netherlands 21 years ago. After having completed school & worked at several jobs ... On 17 December 2012, I founded my first company: investment firm Jasko. After a successful first year, I unfortunately had to close that company. After a short period of rest, unemployment and temporary work. I started again as an entrepreneur. On September 1, 2015, I founded establishment Hajro. (We say establishment instead of company, because we do a bit more then just sell stuff. Like providing jobs, donating to 15 different charities, and helping people to live richer.) Since the beginning the core activity is, selling packages of greeting cards, door to door. Nowadays the product range has been expanded. With, among other things, the selling of my 45 books. Part of the royalties of my books are donated to the charity: foundation Giveth Life. My company also has a few services, like consulting and coaching....You can find them at my Author website at www.jasminhajro6.webnode.nl
 on page services.

For more information about my company & the foundation, go to my website : www.hajro. be which is in dutch. The english website is at www.hajro-international.webnode.nl

Victory 5

Hello, how are you doing ? Thank you for choosing one of my books to read... Have you read Victory 1, 2, 3, and 4 ? Let's start with last year… 2020 corona time… I just kept on working all year long… I have been selling packages of greetingcards… for 52 weeks ,last year… I earned about E 5850,- euros I wrote new books and booklets… I wrote : Through the crisis Running out of time In loving memory Actie als strategie Rahima & Idriz Exposium Hajro, story & catalogus My story Word miljonair in sales Wat het beste werkt ? na 7 jaar ondernemen Ondernemen met hersenschadE Productiviteit crash course And the booklet : My little masterpiece and I kept on writing, the other titles I wrote are : Victory 4 I don't feel like writing, says the author Hackers are scouts Being real and true: in times of fake and pretend 100 % sales rule 200 % sales rule 3 Entrepreneurship cursus Quotes for success I also made my author website at www.jasminhajro6.webnode.nl And I made an international english website for my company Hajro at www.hajro-international.webnode.nl

It was a busy year , at the end of 2020 I slept for 3 days….. exhausted… I was disappointed that I hadn't earned more after working that hard….. but then I figured out why… I was just working half days… selling about 3 or 4 hours a day If you work half the time, you get half the pay half the money isn't enough… So My goal is to work more hours, selling door to door... At the beginning of 2021 I translated 3 of my dutch books into english , they are : Tits, how do I write a book ? How to overcome my addiction ? Start your own business & make it successful. In the harsh reality, where nobody cares My medication against hallucinations is working, it still sometimes happens very briefly.. My medications for sleeping also works, I sleep at 12 or 1 oçlock at night… I decided to be free on Sunday… In the past I would sometimes also go out selling on Sunday.. But now it's a mandatory free day My body and mind need to rest. I go for a run about once a week, I used to do it more often, I have to get back into the habit of doing it more often. I got a subsidy for 3 years, of E 650 euros a month which is settled with the earnings of my company.. If I earn 400 euros , I get 250 euro in subidy And I got help with my debts, I am in a program and have a budget coaching session every month and 3 years from now, in 2024 I will be finally debt free That is my victory

… And because of the subsidy I don't need to worry about money.. another victory I have more peace of mind and I gained 4 kg I have visited my sister and her kids almost every Sunday… Last Friday I worked about 3 hours and sold 14 packages of greeting cards, earning E 70,- euros That's the 2nd or 3rd time that that happened… I watched a lot of South Park episodes and it was fun… After that I changed from watching entertainment to watching other videos about entrepreneurship, like the channel Valuetainment on youtube… And recently I have been watching the videos on the channel Coffeezilla, about all kinds of scammers… It seems there is a whole industry of people scamming people From worthless investments to overpriced courses and actors as business owners… It's of course pathetic for the people that are getting scammed a shame especially if they loose their life's savings… Those people make it harder for real entrepreneurs and salespeople, because they make people untrusting…. The only thing I can do is to not make unrealistic claims., offer a 3 month money back guarantee and be open and transparant, with my company and my books.. I am also on the waiting list for a assisted or guided living.. So within a year or so I will be living on my own, leaving my mothers house.. I think I can do it, I can prepare a meal.. I am sorry, that it's short… but that sums up last year I have added more books to this one, they are : Last 10 years Build your Fortune Overcoming tough times the Ultimate Winning Strategy and Recipe for Happiness You can read them on the following pages enjoy and I hope that they help you to live a happier and richer life. Kind regards, Jasmin Hajro

book, Last 10 years

march 14, 2021 Hello how are you doing…? I am doing okej…. You read in my bio that I am originally from Bosnia, where we lived the first 10 years of my life… and when the war started we fled the country to the Netherlands… Where I went to school and after that I had several jobs, mostly manual labor jobs which I didn't like to do but I did it anyway… Because we all need money to live… My parents had divorced in the Netherlands, and I couldn't handle that… In my puberty I started drinking beer and whisky and I also started experimenting with drugs… marihuana, hashish, xtc, speed and coke… I hanged around the wrong crowd, and got into trouble with the law. I went to jail 3 times, in total 8 months, jail for young people, for stealing and fighting… I stole tobacco and fought with the manager of the store who had caught me… Just stupid shit…. I tried to sell hashish but we ended up smoking it ourself…..

I would get a job from an employment agency, do it for a few weeks or months and then I would come in late a few times too often and lose the job…., or I would not show up at all…. One time I used too many drugs and got into a coma, after that I didn't use anymore… I would still drink alcohol… In 2007 I got a job as a dishwasher in the restaurant of Landal Greenparks in city Doetinchem, where I live… I did that for about a year and then I learned to prepare salads and desserts…. And I started working in the kitchen there…. Eventually after 3 or 4 years I learned to prepare dishes of steak and salmon…. I went to school 1 day in the week, the company payed for it, to get a diploma or certificate for being a cook… I still lived with my mother , earned every month and didn't have much expenses, because mama payed most living expenses… I gave her money…. I started to get interested in finance… I read a lot of books and took a couple of home study courses looking for a system to grow my money… I would drink beer about everyday, every evening after work… in 2010 I collapsed…..

I thought if I keep up my drinking habit, I will destroy myself… So I quit drinking alcohol….
Avoided going out to bars and discotheques… where there was booze… In 2011 when I was clean and sober for a while…. At work …..in the kitchen I started hallucinating… severely…. It scared me… I

didn't want to go crazy... The chef would notice it and send me home... For a while I just worked 3 days a week... but that didn't help... I couldn't sleep right, had some sleepless nights.... Before going to work the next day... Eventually I got fired in 2012..... I got a unemployment benefit for about 8 months.... I received about 800 euro monthly ... Then that ended and I was looking for a job.... I didn't want to do the manual labor jobs for the rest of my life... and I also didn't want to work in the kitchen anymore... So I started my own company.... Investment firm Jasko... I invested my own money in mutual funds... I found a few customers and also invested their money.... I payed out the promised 10% annual return to them.... But I only managed 1600 euros in the portfolio.... If I had an return of 10% on it, that is just 160 euros... I couldn't live from that...

I delivered advertizing and newspapers on the side and I wento to work as a manual laborer... to increase my income.... I was broke most of the time.... Eventually I closed the company... Started lokking for work again... visited a lot of companys with my resumee, but not one had a job for me.... My mother couldn't stand it anymore and put me on the street for one night... It was bad.... No money no phone ....no credit... no help nothing.... I slept outside one night on the street.... My sister came back to live with me and my mother... she had a lot of debt....she worked in sales... door to door selling... My bills and debts started to pile up.... It was a tough time for us.... My sister and her boyfriend gave me an opportunity to sell packages of greeting cards door to door... They trained me in selling... and I went out selling, even before I was completely ready.... I knocked on some doors, found a few customers and kept doing it.... Shortly after that I started my 2nd company establishment Hajro that sells packages of greeting cards, door to door... that was on september 1st 2015... I still do that work.... This is my 6th year in being an entrepreneur with my company Hajro... I earned about 100 euros a month in the first year... I learned about 200 euros a month in the 2nd year I earned about 300 euros a month in the 3rd year I earned about 400 euros a month in the 4th year I earned about 480 euros a month in the 5th year... I also wrote a lot of books and booklets in those years...

In the beginning I was scattered with my focus and activity trying to build an online store... then when I got it finished I couldn't pay for the website and it went offline... then I had to start all over again... What I earned was still not enough to pay for living expenses and to move out of the house... Nor could I pay my mother a decent amount every month.... I would still have hallucinations in those years... it was stressful and they made me very paranoid.... I had applied for help from the government for my income... I got rejected about 5 or 6 times.... Eventually in september 2020 I got subsidy approved.... I would get 650 euros a month and my earnings from my company Hajro would be deducted from that.... Finally a bit stability in my finances.... I also got into a program for my debts... and 3 years from now I will be debt free Hooray Finally... About a year ago I received medication for my hallucinations... and it helps.... They don't happen as frequently anymore... I have more peace of mind.... But the help came about 10 years too late... we , as a family have been thru hell I've written this short booklet, to get some things off my chest... I don't know If you can learn anything from it....

Maybe that ""you should ask for help and don't stop until you get it" If you want lifetime employment, get into sales, door to door selling..... Save money, you will always need it.... Be a good person, help others, but help yourself first....

The Recipe for Happiness, introduction

A book has been written about a true story ... About a man who was imprisoned in a concentration camp at the time of Hitler, and happy. So, Happiness has nothing to do with your circumstances. It has everything to do with, your choice to be happy, regardless of circumstances. Choose to be happy. Of course there are touhger times in life, like when someone you love, dies. That's part of life. Those times of grief you just have to go through and process. Processing is best done by talking about it, to get it off your chest regularly. Or by writing about it, if you write down a situation or your feelings about it, then it's on paper, and it is less in your head. Writing is a good outlet. Processing is also done well by: staying busy. Whether that is in your work or your hobby. They say: a rolling stone does not collect moss. So stay busy .... Okay, now you have learned a good lesson about how to better process negative life experiences. But you're here for the Recipe for Happiness, right? Well, the lesson you've learned will help to make the recipe work better for you. Chapter I Here it comes then ... You have probably read a local newspaper, and you regularly check the news. (the daily news on television) Have you noticed that about 99% of it is bad news? Only misery .. If you did not know better, you would think that the whole world is going to perish. If it's a habit for you, to watch the news every day for half an hour ... Have you ever wondered if it's healthy for you? Does it make you happy ? Of course not !

The easiest way to change a habit is by replacing it with a new habit. So from today on, instead of watching the worldly news half an hour a day .... Watch COMEDY for half an hour a day. Mandatory. Every day. Well, now at half past eight in the evening it's not news time, but Comedy time. If you watch comedy, you relax & you laugh. Sounds healthier, doesn't it? Well, laughing every day is easy to do, right? And replacing your old bad habit in this way, with a nice, healthy new habit, is probably easier than you thought. Except that relaxation is good for you, when you laugh, your body makes endorphins. Those are natural happiness substances. Well, after 21 days of daily watching comedy, you will have formed a new habit. So watch Comedy every day. You can watch a lot of standup comedy on Youtube for free. Simple? Sure, but you have to do it, every day, until you don't have to think about it anymore, and you start doing it automatically.

Chapter II Some Happiness Ingredients in a row: - Watch comedy every day, at least one hour. - Eat ice cream, treat someone with an ice cream. - Work out, throw out your frustration by playing tennis or go for a run. – Pee in the yard (and if you get a fine for urinating, laugh your ass off) – Do not worry, life is too short for that (by staying busy, you do not have time to worry) – Hug the people that you love – Go enjoy a cup of coffee or tea – Buy or save a cat or some other pet – When you receive money, immediately save a part of it – Don't let the media scare you, the world is not getting worse, the world is getting better. – Sex, need I say more (when you have sex your body also produces endorphins = those natural happiness substances) Maybe the Recipe for Happiness is different than you had expected.... But that doesn't matter, the point is that it works & that it will help you to live happier. Do it, it is easier then looking with a sour face. Note from the author If you liked this book & got some value from it. Would you then be so kind, please, to recommend it to the people that you know. So that they too can enjoy it and live happier. Thank you very much.

It was my pleasure to write and translate this book (my third one) for you. I hope it helps you to live happier. (I know it will, if you do the things it teaches) And I hope, that we can together make a contribution to more happiness in the world. We can. If you recommend this book and share it. Then I will promote it. And together we will make a contribution to a happier world. I would appreciate it if you would write a short review. Thank you for your effort. Kind regards, Jasmin Hajro

Previeuw Bouw Jouw Fortuin Preview book Build your fortune the Pay yourself first principle It means that when you receive your money, you first pay yourself, by for example, setting aside a tenth. To clarify your result, we will make an example calculation. For example, you earn 3000 euros or dollars per month. And you pay yourself first, in other words: you put aside a tenth (10%) of your income. So you save 300, - euros per month. A year has 12 months, So after 1 year you'll have (12 x 300) = 3600, - euros. After 1 year you have put a whole month's salary aside. If you put aside a tenth every month, how much will you have after 10 years? (3600 x 10) = 36000, - euro. So after 10 years you have 36000 euros or a whole year's salary in your saving account. Later on in this book: Build your Fortune, you'll see how to make that amount that you put aside each month. Grow faster. Preview book Build your Fortune 10% of everything It is important that when you first pay yourself, by setting aside 10%. That you put 10% of everything aside. Of course 10% of your income. But also 10% of the tips if you receive any, also 10% of your surtax, also 10% of the money you receive as a gift, also 10% of your 13th month, also 10% of your bonus, also 10% of your wage increase, also 10% of your tax refund, also 10% of your welcome bonus, also 10% of your holiday pay. No matter from which angle or from whom you receive money, the first thing you do with it, is to pay yourself first. By setting aside a tenth of it. End of preview.

Preview book Moneymaker Moneymaker 3 The bible for entrepreneurs, written by an entrepreneur. So your daily reading. No, it's not about GOD. It says, written by an entrepreneur ..... YOU READ ONLY BOOKS WHICH ARE WRITTEN BY PEOPLE WHO HAVE THEIR OWN COMPANY !! Do you understand ? This way you prevent feeding your mind with BULLSHIT. And that you will model BULLSHIT. By B.S. I mean unproven idea's and theory. So you save yourself time and money. Ok, then a bit about that Entrepreneurial Bible. It is called No Excuses, the Power of self discipline And is written by Brian Tracy And yes, he has his own company. Otherwise his name would not be here. It comes down to self discipline. And self discipline makes you feel very good about yourself. When you exercise, for example, while most people watch TV. When you work on a Saturday, while most people have a weekend. When you take a step towards achieving your goals on Sunday. The above 3 examples require discipline from you. But 1, 3, 5 years from now where will you wind up ? And where will most people wind up ? Have you ever worked a day with pain because your teeth were broken? Have you ever worked with only 2 hours of sleep, the night before? Have you ever worked without having slept the night before? It was probably easier to watch TV then ..... But if I did, then I would be a Bullshitter for you, and not someone who you respect. I disciplined my self and went to work. Oh yeah, buy the entrepreneurial bible. NOW.

Previeuw book Moneymaker Moneymaker 2. Two things that you have to spend your time on daily Which 2 are they? Watch TV and be on Facebook? Without B.S., so: SALES & DIRECT MARKETING If you sell something (sales), then profit comes in. If you become good at (direct marketing), then profit comes in. With marketing you save yourself time while selling. You do not have to explain who you are and what your company does during your presentation. How many hours per working day do you spend on sales? How many hours per working day do You spend on Direct Marketing? WHAT HAPPENS IF YOU ONLY SPEND YOUR WORKINGTIME ON SALES & DIRECT MARKETING ?? Will you have more profits and therefore more money? End of preview

For more information about this book by me, go to my website : www.jasminhajro.com

Small introduction with establishment Hajro Establishment Hajro is committed to helping the people in the province of Gelderland, by providing jobs and keeping people working, by donating to Charities, and by helping people to live richer. Today Hajro has a few subsidiaries. We now have several products & services, and we support more than 15 charities
(used to be 40 charities). Visit us at www.hajro- international.webnode.nl

 and discover what else we can do for you. Hopefully you will become a raving fan & customer of us. However you choose, I wish you a lot of prosperity & happiness.

Kind regards, Jasmin Hajro

P.S. If you want to let me know your experience with my book. Send me a message by email to j.hajro@hotmail.com. Thanx

My Author Website is at www.jasminhajro6.webnode.nl

You are welcome to visit, I will give you 10 free ebooks there See you soon

P.S.S. I hope you liked my books,
please visit me at my new author website
www.jasminhajro.com
for ways of connecting with me
and lots of discounted books
for you to read.
See you there
Kind regards,
Jasmin Hajro

More books by Jasmin Hajro :
My bibliography....
the books that I have written....
(there are more than 43 titles plus the translations plus the boxsets, so I will only name my english titles)

Build Your Fortune
Moneymaker
Recipe For Happiness
 the Lifebuoy For Banks "Loyal Banking"
the Ultimate Winning Strategy, for entrepreneurs (which is for salespeople & business owners too)

Poems, jokes and book
Victory 1
Victory 2
Always employment & always money in your pocket, everyday.
Things You Don't Want To Know.
Challenges in having your own business, in real life.
how to Grow your money & Build a good retirement in 2 hours per month, for moms, dads, career women and busy people .

Overcoming tough times.
Secrets of writing and selling books.
Double your profits.
Double your profits, extended.
Triumph 1 (boxset)
 Triumph 2 (boxset)

Victorious series (boxset)

Through the crisis
Victory 3
My story
My little masterpiece
Victory 4
I don't feel like writing, says the author
Hackers are scouts
Being real and true: in times of fake and pretend

100 % sales rule
Quotes for success
Entrepreneurship course
3
Last 10 years
Unknown millionaire

At Lulu, where you learn more about the book and where you can buy it as paperback or ebook. Go to www.lulu.com/spotlight/jasminhajro
All my titles are there, but you can search the one that you want.. " I have good experiences ordering at Lulu")

Only available at Amazon and free with Kindle Unlimited are my books :
Lifechanging quotes the
Jasmin Hajro lifestory(which includes Victory 1,2,3,4)
Controversial
This is how you get rich: passively
200 % sales rule

Visit my author website and get 10 free books at www.jasminhajro6.webnode.nl

Note : Over the years a few websites have changed…. My author website is now and will always be at www.jasminhajro6.webnode.nl
You get 10 free books if you visit me there..

My companys website (in dutch) is www.hajro.be
My companys International website (in english) is : www.hajro-international.webnode.nl
You are welcome to visit, maybe there is another great book or great service for yourself waiting there.

Thank you for choosing one of my books to read. Hopefully you are willing to rate it 4 or 5 starting and give it a positive review. Thank you so much for your effort. I will continue to sell greeting cards and write more books until retirement, so more good stuff will be available at my Author website, www.jasminhajro6.webnode.nl
make sure that you visit it every year or more often than that.

Kind regards, Jasmin Hajro

P.S. I hope this book helps you to change your life..

www.ingramcontent.com/pod-product-compliance
Lightning Source LLC
Chambersburg PA
CBHW062354220526
45472CB00008B/1804